The Prayer Habit

Adoration
Confession
Thanksgiving
Supplication

Lilly Lester

SERENITY PUBLISHING & COMMUNICATIONS
P. O. Box 282282
Nashville. TN 37228
(404) 608-2416

ISBN 0-9712701-7-1

To God Be The Glory

The Prayer Habit

60 Daily Meditations

Introduction

The Prayer Habit was birthed out of a desire to become disciplined in prayer, after recommitting my life to Christ. Praying my personal cause was no longer an option. Praying without ceasing became my goal. However, I felt I didn't know how, that I was unworthy, and that God would not hear me. Times of prayer became times of frustration and struggle. Trying to think of something profound to say and keeping my mind focused became harder and harder. Until I learned that prayer is not a performance, but, just simply coming to God with a sincere heart and communicating with Him. Acknowledging who He is, touching Him in prayer and allowing Him to touch me with His love. Praising and worshipping Him, sharing my situations, making my request known and listening for Him to speak. Praying in faith. Acknowledging that the power is His, the privilege is mine.

The sin of prayerlessness is as common as any other sin, sad to say, even among Christians. Satan has been successful in keeping us ignorant and blind because of our muchness and busyness. The spiritual discipline of prayer must take precedence over every thing and every person, if we are to be victorious in every area of our lives.

The acronym ACTS (Adoration, Confession, Thanksgiving and Supplication) guides you into the habit of praying to the Lord on a consistent basis. Meditating on the Prayer Habit will bring about a desire to delve deeper into your own personal prayers. You may begin after 60 days to pray your own ACTS in section II of the Prayer Habit. This time of drawing near to God as He draws near to you, will become habit forming and you can become one of God's secret agents through the prayer habit.

Preface

The Prayer Habit focuses on only one component of prayer, the ACTS. It is uniquely designed for those that desire to come into an intimate prayer relationship with the Father, yet find it difficult to be consistent. Jesus' life was a disciplined life of prayer and the power of God flowed out from Him. Forming the habit of a consistent, daily prayer time also requires discipline. And we too can experience the power of God flowing out from us. The ACTS provides a jump start of the prayer habit.

Beginning with adoration. Adoring, worshipping, and praising the wonder and glory of God's divine character. Acknowledging who He is and His mighty acts. Confession is essential to the believer's relationship with God and with others. Confession allows us to acknowledge our sins and receive forgiveness as we come into agreement with God. Thanksgiving begins by acknowledging who God is and what He has done. The ACTS cultivates a heart of gratitude consistently. Supplication prayer is transferring in earnestness our petitions before the Lord, and trusting Him to meet the need.

The Prayer Habit teaches us to focus on the awesomeness of God. It will help to build your faith as you spend time with the Father, which will lead to a habit forming lifestyle of prayer when we become doers of the Word. I Thess. 5:17 "Pray without ceasing." Romans 12:12 indicates, we should be "continuing steadfastly in prayer." Be empowered through the prayer habit.

Forming the Habit....

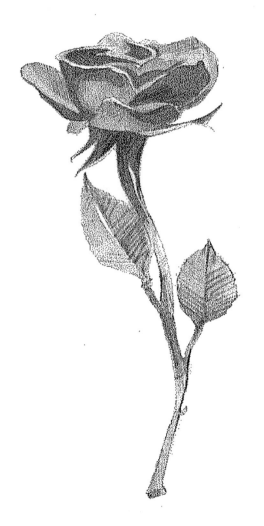

Adoration

Both riches and honor come from You, and You reign over all.
In Your hand is power and might.
In Your hand it is to make great and to give strength to all.
Now therefore, our God.
We thank You and praise Your glorious name.
I Chron. 29: 12, 13

Confession

Forgive me for an adulterous relationship with You. At times, I have courted the enemy. Right now, I renounce Satan in the name of Jesus. The work of darkness holds no power over me because "Greater is He that is in me, than he that is in the world."
I John 4:4

Thanksgiving

Thank You, that You are the Ancient of Days, the God that never changes, who supplies all of our needs according to Your riches in glory. Thank You for the ancient path of wisdom and revelation knowledge.

Supplication

Enlighten the eyes of my understanding that I may know the hope of Your calling in my heart.

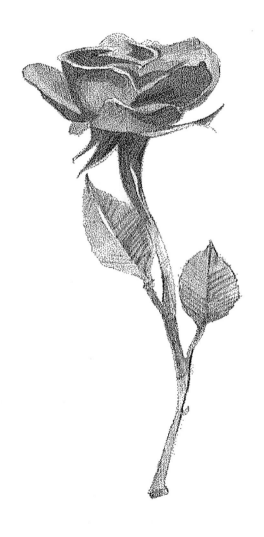

Adoration

Bless the Lord, O my soul;
And all that is within me, bless His holy name.
Psalms 103:1

Confession

I confess that sometimes my blessings to You have been half
hearted. Forgive me, and teach me how to worship and praise
You in spirit and in truth.

Thanksgiving

For every benefit;
Who forgiveth all my iniquities,
Who healeth all my diseases,
Who crowneth me with loving kindness and tender mercies,
Who satisfieth my mouth with good things, so that my mouth
is renewed like the eagles.
Psalms 103:2-5

Supplication

Give me, O Lord, a broken and contrite spirit. That my will,
will become Yours deliberately. Let my joy come from seeking
to please You.

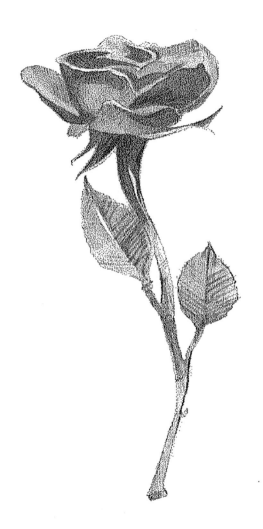

Adoration

You, and You alone are my only God. My heart overflows with
love for You. I long to be
in Your presence. My spirit soars as I ponder on Your magnifi-
cence. I am overwhelmed as
I approach Your holiness.

Confession

Lord, I confess that I have sometimes worshipped and made
gods out of the wrong things
and even sometimes people. I forsake all idols and ask your
forgiveness. Come into my heart and make my heart your
home.

Thanksgiving

Thank You, that our boast is made in You and not in worthless
idols. Because of Your
grace, mercy, and love towards us, what idol can compare to
Your awesomeness.

Supplication

Do not incline my heart to any evil thing, O Lord, let me not
practice the works of the
wicked.
Psalm 141:4

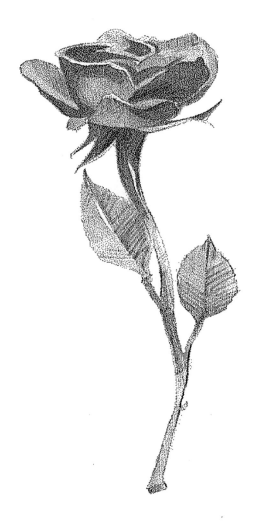

Adoration

You shaped and formed me before the foundation of the world,
to love, honor, and to
reverence You. I love You with my whole heart. I honor Your
majesty. I reverence You for
Your mighty acts and wondrous works, Almighty and Everlasting God.

Confession

Lord, how can I love You and not like me. Teach me who I am
in You so that my love for
You will be unshakeable. And I will be confident in who I am
in Christ.

Thanksgiving

For it is in You, that we live, move and have our being. We
affirm that we can do
absolutely nothing without Your grace. We do not attempt to
take your love for granted. Thank you for Your endless love.

Supplication

Inspire us to encourage others more and think less of ourselves.

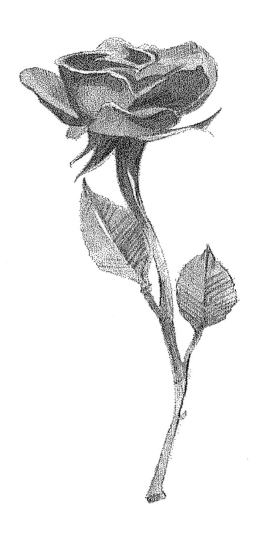

Adoration

All glory, praise, honor, blessing, power, and strength to my
Savior and my Lord for He
hath done great things for me.

Confession

When I lose my focus while majoring on my circumstances,
You seem so far away.
Forgive me for relying on my emotions. Give me I pray, an
unwavering faith instead.

Thanksgiving

God of all comfort. Thank You for calming my anxious heart
and bringing comfort to my
soul. Knowing that I can put all my trust in You gives me inner
peace and assurance.

Supplication

Do not hide Your face from me;
Do not turn Your servant away in anger;
You have been my help;
Do not leave me nor forsake me,
O God of my salvation
Psalm 27:9

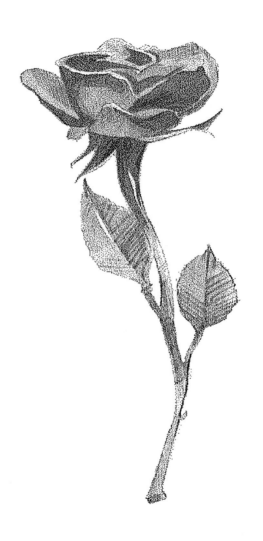

Adoration

I will extol You, my God, O king and I will bless Your name
forever and ever. Everyday I will bless You, and will praise Your
name forever and ever.

Psalm 145:1,2

Confession

Time is so precious, yet I am guilty of not using it wisely.
Forgive me for inconsistency
in my times with You. Teach me how to redeem the time.

Thanksgiving

Lord, I thank You for every hour in the day. Thank You for
family time, leisure time,
workplace time, rest time, and time in Your presence.

Supplication

Teach me Lord to organize my time for Your glory.

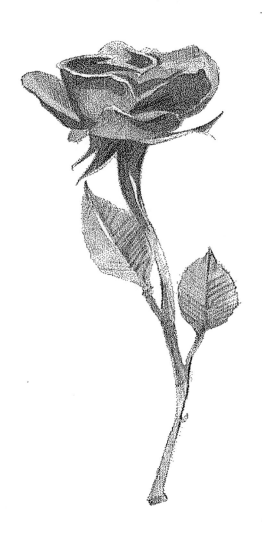

Adoration

O Lord, how majestic is Your name in all the earth, Your name alone brings peace,
comfort, love, healing, gratitude, confession, praise, joy, and worship. How majestic is
Your name in all the earth. I hallow the name, that is above every name.

Confession

Pardon me when I have not reverenced Your holy name. "Jesus"

Thanksgiving

For the power and authority in the name of Jesus, thank You.

Supplication

Inspire me to reverence Your name at all times, in all places and in all situations.

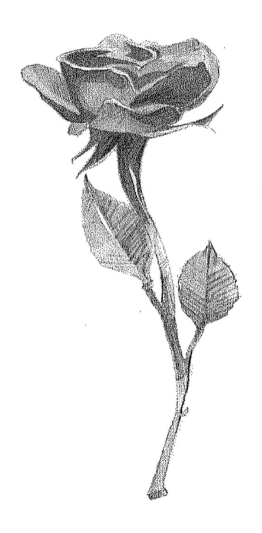

Adoration

When I remember the wonderful works Your hands have wrought, my heart overflows with Adoration, Confession and Thanksgiving.

Confession

When I have overlooked Your good works and chased pride, power and position to appease me for a season, forgive me O Lord. Forgive my ignorance of forgetting who I am and what I have in Christ Jesus.

Thanksgiving

Because I am Your workmanship, created in Christ Jesus for good works, which You have prepared beforehand that I should walk in them. I thank You.
Ephesians 2:10

Supplication

Teach me, I pray to say no to ungodliness and worldly passion. Teach me to live a self controlled and upright life, that I may bring honor and glory to You all the days of my life.

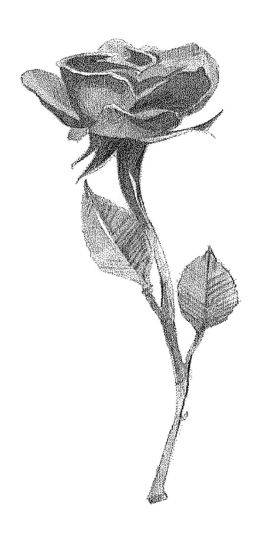

Adoration

O come, let us adore Him, You light the path of Holiness, is it any wonder that we adore You? O come let us adore Him, Christ our King.

Confession

Discipline becomes drudgery when it is not a priority. Forgive me, I pray for not exercising the spiritual disciplines on a consistent basis in my spiritual walk. Birth in me a passion to be disciplined in every area of my life.

Thanksgiving

Thank You for giving us the blueprint to live a disciplined life. Thank You that Your word trains, instructs, and disciplines.

Supplication

Show me the path of life; I pray, that I may live a blameless life before You.

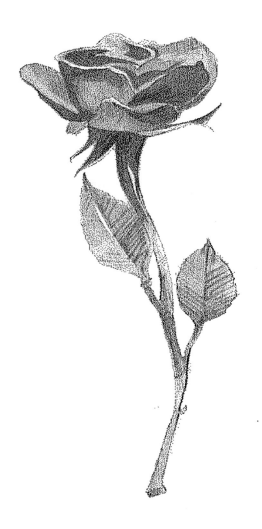

Adoration

You, O Lord have been my dwelling place, therefore, I will adore You, magnify You, extol You, exalt You, and glorify You with all that is within me.

Confession

I confess Lord, that I have been comfortable dwelling in darkness. Glorifying the wrong things. According to Your loving kindness; according to the multitude of Your tender mercies. Blot out my transgression and lead me to dwell in the light of Your love.

Thanksgiving

Thank You Lord for teaching me to crucify my sinful nature with its ungodly desires. I will delight myself in You and meditate on Your word day and night, therefore, I do not gratify my sinful nature which is contrary to the spirit. Thank You for the Holy Spirit.

Supplication

Create in me a clean heart, O God, and renew a steadfast spirit within me.
Psalm 51:10

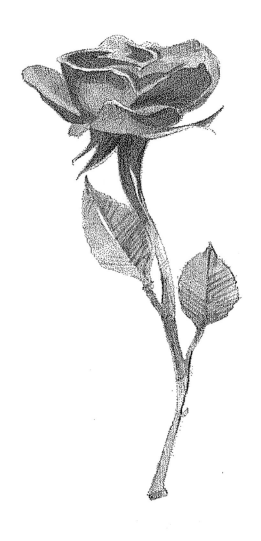

Adoration

Your glory awakens me. Your glory surrounds me all the day. Your glory keeps me throughout the night. Your glory invokes me to praise and causes me to sing "How Great Thou Art". For You are the greater one. I adore You. I worship You.

Confession

For the secret sins that would make me feel unaccepted and ashamed, cleanse and deliver me, I pray, teach me to cast down anything that enters my mind that is unholy and leaves a stench in Your nostrils.

Thanksgiving

When the enemy would try to disturb my spirit, and invade my thoughts. You still my very soul and mind when I think on the name "*Jesus*." Thank You for Your peace.

Supplication

Give heed to the voice of my cry,
My King and my God,
For to You I will pray,
My voice You shall hear in the morning, O Lord.
In the morning I will direct it to You.
And I will look up.
Psalm 5:2-3

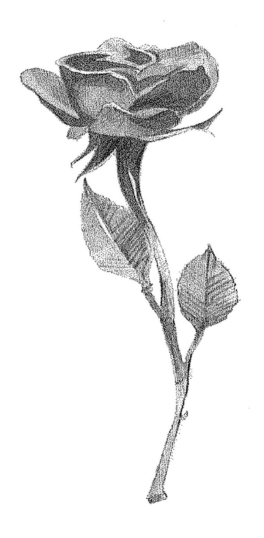

Adoration

O God, there is no life aside from You, there is nothing but emptiness, but in You, my heart is filled to overflowing because of Your love, Your grace, and Your mercy. O how I love You.

Confession

Lord, because I have looked for peace and love in all the wrong places. There is a void in me that only You can fill. Send Your word that I might be filled. I give my heart to You this day.

Thanksgiving

For quickening Your word in my heart that I might live it out in total commitment and in obedience to You. I thank You, I will bless Your name forever.

Supplication

Enable me Lord Jesus to stand fast in You , and hold fast to what is good. Impart into me strength and courage that I may do all things to Your glory.

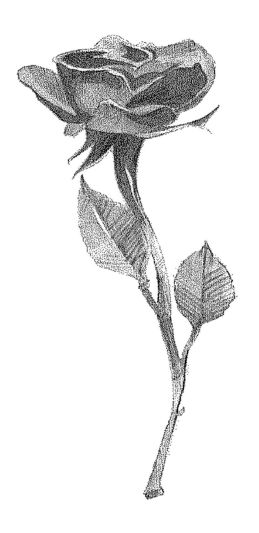

Adoration

Without Your stubborn love, where would I be? Because it has never let go of me. I love You, I adore You, I praise You. I will bless You all the day of my life.

Confession

I turn to You in my stubbornness, Oh God, I accept Your invitation to quench my thirst. I confess that I have bought that which is not good. Forgive me for leaning to my own understanding and not seeking Your way.

Thanksgiving

Thank You Father, for inviting me to Your table to eat that which is good, that my soul might delight itself in Your fatness.

Supplication

Teach me to feast on spiritual things, and to hearken diligently unto You.

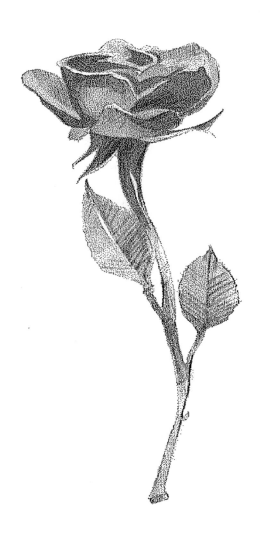

Adoration

Thou art exalted high above all the earth. Your thoughts, Your ways, Your plans are high above all the earth. I exalt thee, Oh Lord. I lift my hands to You. I will praise You for You are exalted above all the earth.

Confession

Many times I have not exalted Your name in the home, in the marketplace, even in the church, forgive me for busyness, indifference, or just plain ungratefulness. I pray.

Thanksgiving

For loving me in spite of the times I have exalted self. Thank You for withholding Your wrath from a wretch like me.

Supplication

Teach me Father to love the things that You love, and to despise the things that You despise.

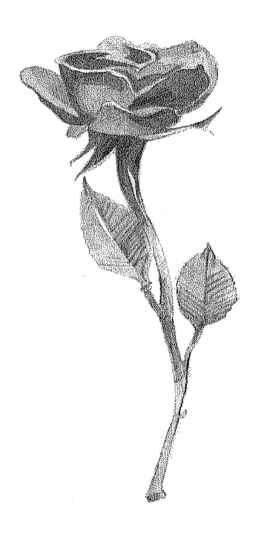

Adoration

In the silence of the early hours, I join in with nature to praise You, is there any wonder, my soul cries out "Early will I seek You. Early will I love You. Early will I honor You."

Confession

Character does not always boast itself, but is always evidenced by my thoughts, words and deeds. Forgive me, when my character reflected a distorted image of You.

Thanksgiving

For giving us things to concentrate on that will build character and will result in right living and peace. Things that are true, noble, just, pure, lovely and of good report. Thank You Lord.
Philippians 4:8

Supplication

Inspire me to strive to possess the character of Christ. Teach me to examine my fruit by Christ's example.

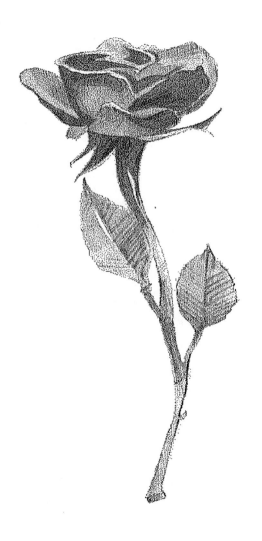

Adoration

Yours, O Lord, is the greatness, the power, and the glory, the victory and the majesty; for all that is in heaven and in earth is Yours, Yours is the kingdom, O Lord, and You are exalted as head over all.
I Chron. 29:11

Confession

For the times I have been influenced by the world, and not by Your Holy Spirit forgive me. When I have been influenced by self confidence and not God confidence, forgive me I pray.

Thanksgiving

Because you are a loving Father, working out everything for my good I am blessed even in adversity. Thank You that Your mercy endureth forever.

Supplication

Let my feet neither slip nor stumble, order my steps, I pray and keep me on a straight path.

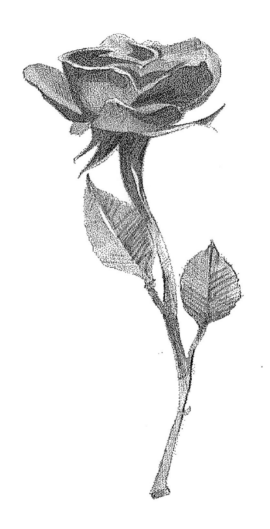

Adoration

For the gift of Your precious Son, for the blood that cleanses and heals my tainted soul, for adopting me into the family of God I adore You. I love You, I will forever sing Your praises.

Confession

I confess, because there is no good thing in me, deliver me from the sins to which I am most prone. Help me to set my mind on things above and not on things of this earth.

Thanksgiving

My flesh and my heart may fail; but God is the strength of my heart and my portion forever.
Psalm 73:26

Supplication

Do not cast me off in the time of old age. Do not forsake me when my strength fails.

Psalm 70:9

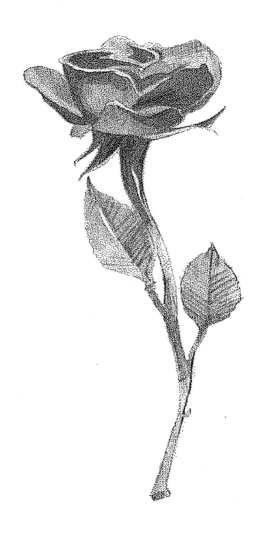

Adoration

I chime in with Your angels to sing Holy, Holy, Holy, no sooner than I finish You've blessed me again and I sing Holy, Holy, Holy, only to discover You keep on blessing me, and I sing again Holy, Holy, Holy in the inner recesses of my heart all the day.

Confession

Maintain in me a hunger for holiness. I pray that I will decrease that You may increase in me.

Thanksgiving

Today I am blessed with all spiritual blessings, I am especially thankful for my silent partner that leads me, and teaches me in all things.

Supplication

Teach me, I pray to give of myself for Your service. Teach me, O God, to walk before You in holiness.

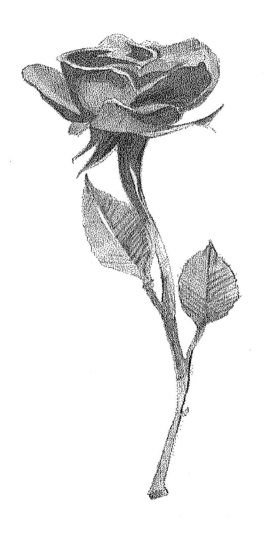

Adoration

For shedding Your grace on this great country, we love You, we magnify You, we glorify You, we praise You, we will worship You on this holy ground You have blessed us with, all our days on earth.

Confession

Forgive us for the times we have not treated the good earth as holy ground. Forgive us for not seeing all things in the good earth as good.

Thanksgiving

For making all things in the earth good. For food, shelter, raiment and success. For crowning our good with brotherhood, for this great country of America, we thank you. God, our Father.

Supplication

Teach us Lord, to be good stewards over all You have blessed us with in the earth.

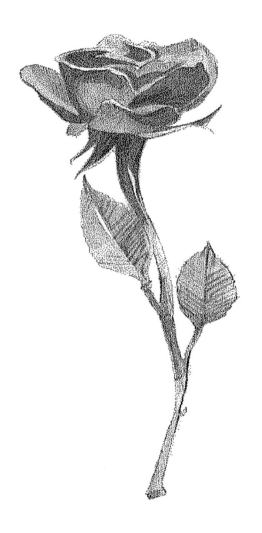

Adoration

I adore You Almighty God for Your great and marvelous works.
Just, tried, and true are Your ways. Who can compare to my
God? Who is Worthy? None but the infinite God Himself.

Confession

When I have not reverenced You in my conversation, my deeds,
and in my thoughts it has caused me to make unwise choices,
because of lack of wisdom. Forgive me, I pray, for leaning, to
my own understanding and making a mess.

Thanksgiving

Thank You for Your grace and Your mercy, You grace me to
face and go through situations that I know I could not handle
on my own. Your mercy gives me another chance to right
wrong.. Thank you Jesus!

Supplication

Turn me away from my self indulgent life. Teach me to die
daily to self.

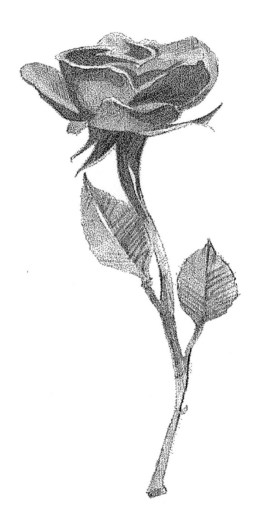

Adoration

O Great Light you who have shone out of the darkness. You who shines in our hearts to give knowledge, wisdom and understanding. How we adore thee.

Confession

I must confess, I have not always loved my neighbor as myself, or seen my neighbor as God sees them. Forgive me and teach me to look at my neighbor with the same love that God looks at me.

Thanksgiving

The ultimate love relationship is in Christ Jesus. The relationship is one of unconditional love. He loves me "as is". Thank You Jesus that You see right through me, yet You keep on loving me.

Supplication

Keep me as the apple of your eye;
Hide me under the shadow of your wings.
From the wicked who oppress me.
From the deadly enemies who surround me.
Psalm 17:8-9

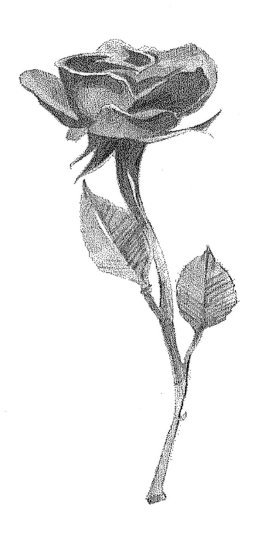

Adoration

My altar is before You, O God, not filled with unclean offerings, or with incense but rather, filled with righteousness, praise, love, and joy waiting to be offered up to You. Because I love and adore You.

Confession

In the name of Jesus, I pray that my destiny becomes not my destruction, nor my stomach my God, nor my desires, my shame, create in me a clean heart, as my mind becomes renewed in You.

Thanksgiving

Thank you, that You have turned my mourning into dancing. You have put off my sackcloth and clothed me with gladness. To the end that my glory may sing praise to You and not be silent.
O Lord, my God, I will give thanks to You forever.
Psalm 30:11-12

Supplication

Know my soul in adversities, I pray, O God be my helper.

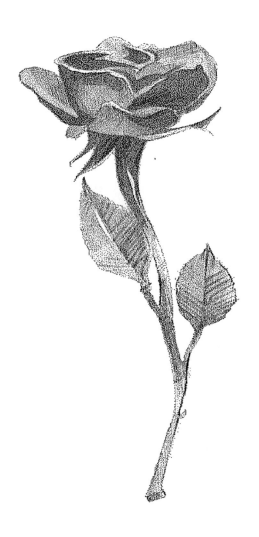

Adoration

The Lord is my strength and my shield, my heart trusted in
Him and I am helped; my heart greatly rejoices, and with my
song I will praise Him.
Psalm 28:7

Confession

I confess the law of the Lord is perfect, converting the soul;
the testimony of the Lord is sure, making wise the simple.
Psalm 19:7

Thanksgiving

Yet in all these things we are more than conquerors through
Him who loved us.
Romans 8:37
Thank You, Father, I do not have a failure mentality, but the
mind of Christ.

Supplication

Empower me to endure my sufferings as a good soldier and to
meet every challenge knowing and acknowledging that You are
in control.

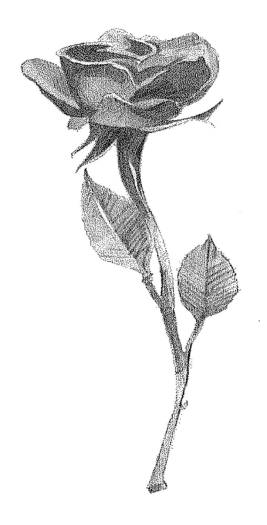

Adoration

The trees and their leaves speak to me of Your blessings in abundance. The raindrops speak to me of Your laughter, storms speak to me of Your power, the sun speaks to me of Your love. Your spirit speaks to me of Your grace. Your glory speaks to me of Your Holiness.

Confession

I confess there was a time when I was afraid of Your presence. Not sure what it would be like, but today I confess it is gloriously transforming from the old, to a new way of abundant living.

Thanksgiving

When I come into Your presence, light begins to dispel darkness, a warmth envelopes me. I wait eagerly for You to meet me. I wait prayerfully and silently. I feel like a newborn babe nestled on its mothers breast peacefully sleeping.

Supplication

Rekindle afresh the fires that once burned so brightly for You, ignite me with a new desire to love You more deeply than before.

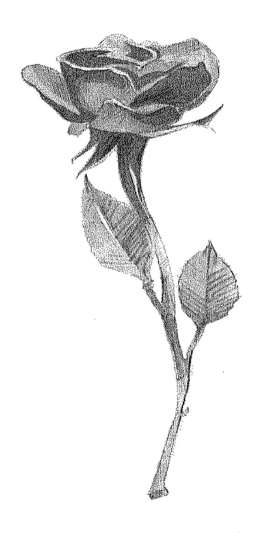

Adoration

In the stillness of the early morning, Your presence surrounds me, Your peace gently flows through me, Your warmth envelopes me, and a small voice speaks to me saying, "Be still and know that I am God." My heart is still and I am lost in Your presence, in the glory of the one I love. And my spirit, soul, and body rejoices with love for You.

Confession

When I have been too hurried to linger in Your presence, too hurried to hear Your final word, too hurried to be blessed abundantly, forgive me.

Thanksgiving

"Thy will be done" is my prayer and my utmost desire. Thank You that in Your will, I will neither falter nor fail.

Supplication

Lord, all my longings are known to You. Do not forsake me Lord; O my God, do not be far from me. Make haste to help me, O lord my salvation.

Adoration

Not unto us Lord, not unto us, but to Your name give glory,
Because of Your mercy,
Because of Your truth.
Psalm 115:1

Confession

I confess that my thoughts and my deeds are not always pure,
forgive me, for walking in the flesh and not in the spirit.

Thanksgiving

Let them sacrifice the sacrifices of thanksgiving. And declare
His works with rejoicing.

Psalm 107:22

Supplication

Teach us to put to death, whatever in us that is fleshly; fornica-
tion, impurity, evil desires and greed, that we may glorify You
in all that we do.

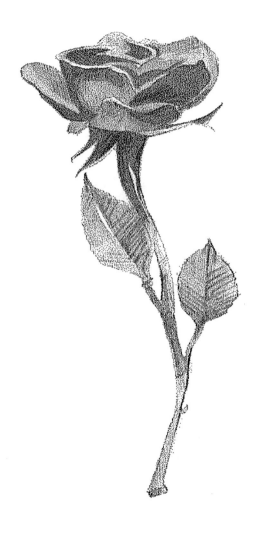

Adoration

Ascribe power to God, whose majesty is in all the earth, marvelous are His works. Awesome is God in His sanctuary. We adore and glorify You, for You alone are worthy.

Confession

Pardon me when the light of Your son Jesus Christ could not shine through me. Dispel the darkness. I pray that the light of Christ will become a beacon in me for those who grope in darkness to see.

Thanksgiving

All your works shall give thanks to You, O Lord and all Your faithful shall bless You. They shall speak of the glory of Your kingdom, and tell of Your power, to make known to all people Your mighty deeds. Thank You that your kingdom is an ever-lasting kingdom and Your dominion endures throughout all generations.

Psalm 145:10-13

Supplication

Teach me, I pray to walk in Your way, and to do Your will for Your praise, and glory.

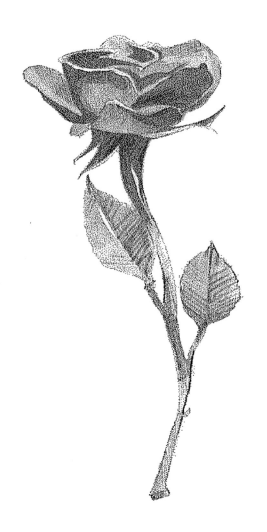

Adoration

You alone are my all sufficient one, I see You in the twinkling eyes of the children, I hear You speak love through their words of love. I feel Your warmth as they embrace me. I rejoice in Your love today. For You are love supreme, love glorified, love magnified. You are love.

Confession

Forgive me for my busyness and muchness with the cares of life. Forgive me for being too shallow to see Your beauty and majestic touch in everything through a child's eyes.

Thanksgiving

Thank You God for expressing Your love through a child, the honesty and sincerity of a child saying "I love you" or grasping my hand warms my heart, and I know it is You stroking me ever so gently.

Supplication

Teach me, I pray, to trust You for everything as a child trusts a mother and father to meet their needs and to protect them.

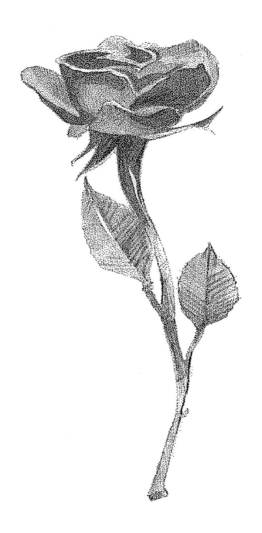

Adoration

The wind of Your presence, awakens my senses, Your fragrance
is soft and delicate to my nostrils, Your touch so gentle and
comforting, Your sound sweet music to my ears, Your taste
sweeter than honeycomb. I see Your glory throughout the earth
and I breathtakingly whisper "I love You."

Confession

Forgive me when I have boasted in self, and not in Your sufferings. My sins have made my heart heavy. Cleanse me, purge me,
that I may bring forth good fruit, to Your glory.

Thanksgiving

For keeping my faith alive in You, I thank you.

Supplication

Teach me to walk by faith, and not by sight.

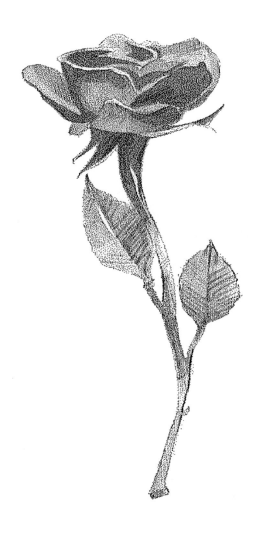

Adoration

Yes Lord, I will give thanks to You, I will sing praises to Your
name, O most High; I will declare Your loving kindness in the
morning, and Your faithfulness every night.
Psalm 92:1-2

Confession

Pardon me, for the times when I have not been a faithful stew-
ard over the things that You given me charge over. The large
and small things, and especially the spiritual blessings. Forgive
me.

Thanksgiving

Thank You for the many blessings in my life, salvation, family,
health, friends, a good name, holy leisure, opportunity, and all
the things that make me rich without money.

Supplication

Assist me in the ordering of my private life, that I may truly be
a Godly example to all with whom I come in contact with
today.

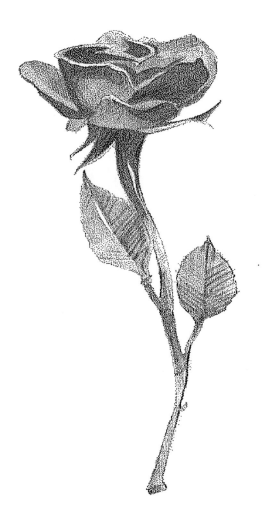

Adoration

Almighty God, we adore You today as the glorious one, the giver of light and life, creator and shaper of all things, the one who sustains and loves us. We adore You, for You have done great and marvelous things.

Confession

I will fear not, for You are with me; I will not be dismayed for You are my God. You will strengthen and help me. You will uphold me with Your righteous right hand.
Isaiah 41:9-10

Thanksgiving

For the purity and innocence of the little ones that You have given me to nurture, train, and love, "Thank you," I will train them in the fear and admonition of the Lord all of my days.

Supplication

Give me a teachable spirit and a yielded heart, O Lord.

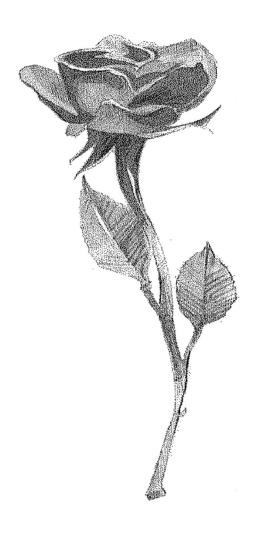

Adoration

I will mention the loving kindness of the Lord and the praises
of the Lord, according to all the Lord has bestowed on us.
Isaiah 63:7

Confession

Lord, I am guilty of not mentioning Your loving kindness
enough. Help me to never forget that it is in You that I live,
move and have my being. My lips shall praise You in the gates
forever.

Thanksgiving

For the oil of gladness instead of mourning, for the garment of
praise instead of depression, that I am not forsaken and neither
am I shaken. I thank you that I am strong in the Lord and in the
power of His might.

Supplication

Inspire me Lord, to keep my mind renewed with Your word,
inspire me to desire the mind of Christ, inspire me to seek the
spirit of wisdom and revelation in the knowledge of You,
through Your holy spirit, inspire me.

Adoration

Without Your grace where would I be? Without Your mercy who would I be? Because of Your great love for me, I am made new. I am the righteousness of Christ, I am alive with Your light. I live to praise You.

Confession

Forgive me for not following Your example, forgiving, and doing unto others as I would have them do unto me.

Thanksgiving

For the spiritual gifts that You have placed in me to further kingdom building on earth, Lord, I thank you.

Supplication

Stir up the gifts that You have blessed me with, that I may be obedient to the great commission that You have commanded me to do.

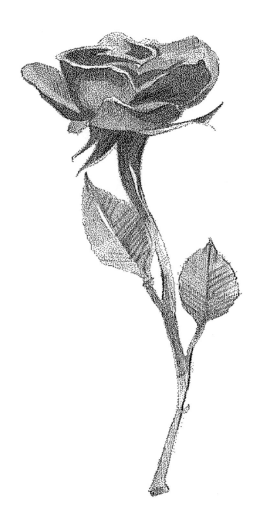

Adoration

The embrace of Your arms around me as I whisper Your name is wonderful, all of my senses are stirred as I whisper from the depth of my inner being. "Jesus."

Confession

When things are not going like I think they should, I sometimes try to help You, even if it means a little manipulation or a little control here and there. I repent from the spirit of manipulation, and control that would attach itself to me.

Thanksgiving

Thank You that your thoughts are not our thoughts, neither are Your ways our ways. Thank You that Your ways are higher than our ways and Your thoughts higher than our thoughts.

Supplication

Give me, I pray the faith to stand still and see the salvation of the Lord.

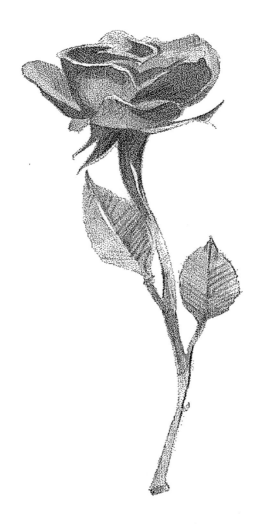

Adoration

I will praise You O Lord, for You have caused me to overcome
and triumph mightily in my distress and sorrow.

Confession

For Your name's sake, O Lord, pardon my iniquity, for it is
great.
Psalm 25:11

Thanksgiving

In everything give thanks; for this is the will of God in Christ
Jesus for you.
I Thessalonians 5:18

Supplication

Hear, O Lord, when I cry with my voice!
Psalm 27:7

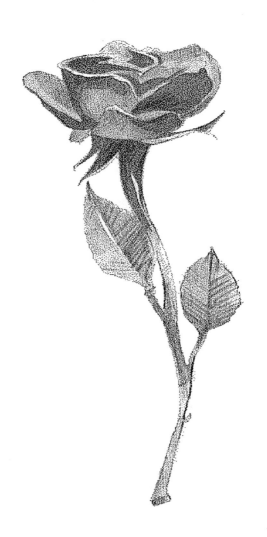

Adoration

When I think of the goodness of Jesus, I cannot help but adore, cherish, respect and praise You. My spirit, soul and body say "yes Lord."

Confession

I confess entertaining carnality, forgive me for insensitivity to the Holy Spirit. Season my words with Your grace.

Thanksgiving

Jesus giver of all life. I thank You for the light of life in Christ, the life that only You can give, that causes rivers of living waters to flow from us, that others may see You in us and be provoked to jealousy.

Supplication

Teach me to seek Your presence continuously, O Lord my God.

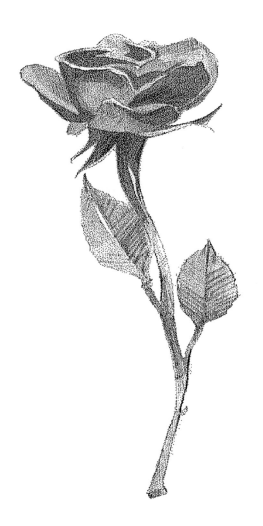

Adoration

Great is Your love, mercy, and grace toward me. When I look at Your heavens, the work of Your fingers, the moon and the stars that You have established, what are human beings that You are mindful of them, mortals that You care for them?
Psalm 8:3-4

Confession

You have made me in Your image and crowned me with a touch of Your glory. Forgive me, I pray for not living up to Your glory and honor. Teach me how to glorify You.

Thanksgiving

I will praise You for I am fearfully and wonderfully made. Thank you for making me in Your express image.

Supplication

Keep me in remembrance Lord, that You made me to glorify You and You only.

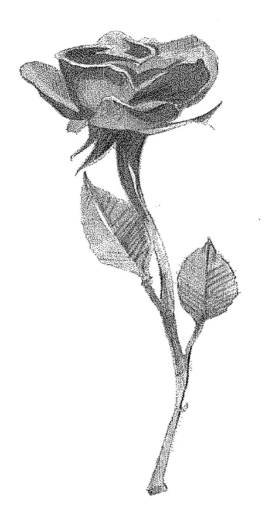

Adoration

O Lord our Lord,
How excellent is Your name in all the earth. Who have set
Your glory above the heavens.
Psalm 8:1

Confession

I confess my spirit is not always teachable, but stubborn and
rebellious, ever learning but not growing in the knowledge of
You. Tear down this will of mine and replace it with "Thy will
be done."

Thanksgiving

Thank You for the promise of eternal life, peace, health, joy,
wisdom, and hope. The
promise that if we abide in Your word and Your word abides in
us we can ask anything of
You in Your name.

Supplication

Give us faith, that we may stand on Your promises without
wavering.

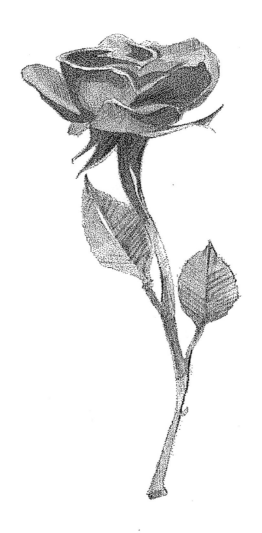

Adoration

We praise You O God, for the love You so freely give to me through Your mercy, grace, faithfulness, compassion and even through Your chastisement. I praise You. I extol You. I exalt You. I behold You as the only true and living God.

Confession

For the atonement for our sins, for the bruises, the stripes, the shame. Forgive me, O God, I confess You as Lord over my life from this day forward, to serve and live for You.

Thanksgiving

O how great is Your goodness.
Which You have laid up for those who fear You,
Which You have prepared for those who trust in You.
In the presence and sons of men.
Thank you for Your goodness.
Psalm 31:19

Supplication

I cried out to You, O Lord.
And to the Lord I made supplication;
What profit is there in my blood, when I go down to the pit?
Will the dust praise You?
Will it declare Your truth?
Hear, O Lord, and have mercy on me;
Lord, be my helper.

Psalm 30:8-10

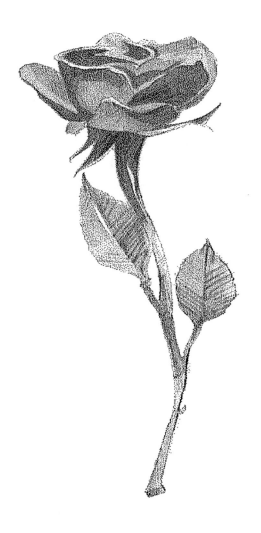

Adoration

For You are my inspiration, you are my song, you are the balm that soothes my soul, and quiets my heart. You are the inexpressible joy that floods through my soul. You are my life line. I love you.

Confession

I confess too much activity and not enough quiet. Develop in me the love for quietness, that I may commune with You and learn to value and appreciate the discipline of silence.

Thanksgiving

Thank You for developing a sensitive ear to the voice of God in me, which must become a daily discipline. Thank You, Holy Spirit for teaching me that silence is a requirement to hearing the voice of God.

Supplication

Teach me to study to be quiet, to do my own business, to work with my own hands that I may walk properly toward those who are outside.
I Thessalonians 4:12

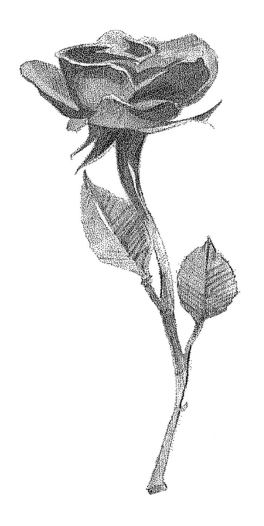

Adoration

He is your praise, and He is your God, who has done for you
these great and awesome things which your eyes have seen.
Deuteronomy 10:12

Confession

Against thee and thee only have I sinned, and done this evil in
Your sight. Forgive me, wash me, that I might be whiter than
snow.
Psalm 51:4,76

Thanksgiving

Let us come before His presence with thanksgiving, Let us
shout joyfully to Him with psalms. For the Lord is the great
God, and the great King above all Gods.
Psalm 95:3

Supplication

Be our refuge and strength, O God. A very present help in
trouble.
Psalm 46:1

Adoration

For Your amazing grace, the unmerited favor that You would grace me with today. How can I help but love and adore You. For Your loving kindness toward mankind. I will magnify and glorify Your name all the days of my life.

Confession

Works of righteousness I have not always done. Today I renounce the works of darkness, I choose light. I ask Your forgiveness for wrong choices on this day. Guide me aright I pray.

Thanksgiving

Because I am no longer under law, but under grace, Lord I thank You. Your grace is sufficient for me and causes me to choose works of righteousness over works of darkness.

Supplication

Empower me Lord, to choose to do the works of righteousness, and to reverence You as You work in me.

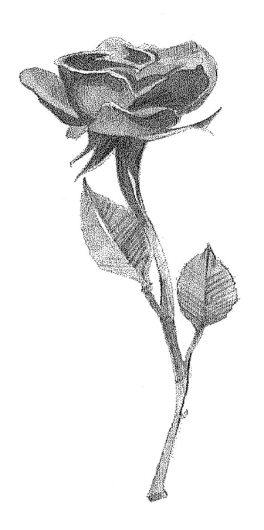

Adoration

Holy, Holy, Holy, I will bless Your name in all the earth, because You are holy, holy, holy. Precious is Your name to all that call upon it. Holy, holy, holy. Holy is the Lord.

Confession

Faithful and true You are, therefore, I will come boldly to Your throne, to confess my sins and ask for Your forgiveness in Jesus' name.

Thanksgiving

Because You alone are the lifter up of my head, I thank You.

Supplication

Great and awesome God,
Let the words of my mouth and the meditation of my heart be acceptable to You, O Lord my strength and my redeemer.
Psalm 19:14

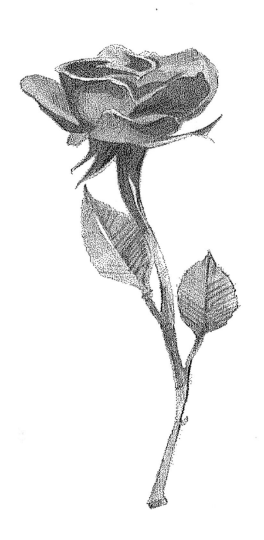

Adoration

I will bless the Lord at all times. His praise shall continually be in my mouth.
Psalm 34:1

Confession

Lord, sometimes we get too busy to bless You. Give us we pray, a holy desire to lead a life of allegiance to You, set apart and surrendered.

Thanksgiving

Thank You as we yield our lives to You through prayer, meditation on your word, and obedience. Thank you that our spirit man is strengthened and the character of our outward man represents Christ Jesus.

Supplication

May we be found blameless until the coming of our Lord Jesus Christ.

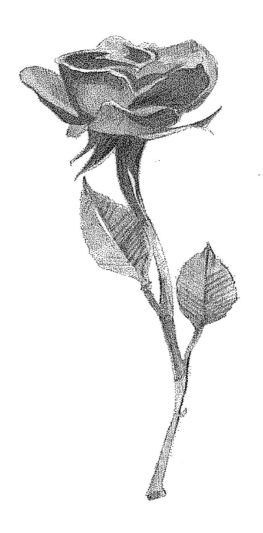

Adoration

Almighty and Everlasting God, I long to know You personally. I long to know You so intimately that I feel Your heart beat. I long to think Your thoughts, esteem the things You esteem and hate the things You hate. Just because I love and adore You.

Confession

For the times when my way seemed right in my own eyes. The times I chose to lean to my own understanding, I repent. Lead me, I pray, to do justice and righteousness that my sacrifice might be acceptable to You.

Thanksgiving

You are my rock and my fortress and my deliverance; The God of my strength in whom I will trust; My shield and horn of my salvation, my stronghold and my refuge; My Savior, You save me from violence.
2 Samuel 22:2-3

Supplication

Lord, help me to know You as Protector today.

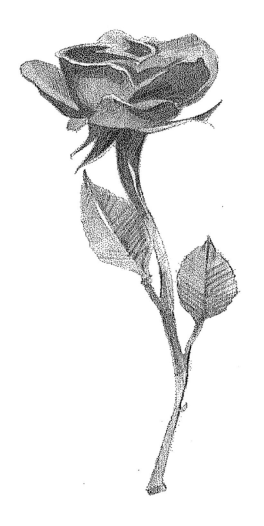

Adoration

"I will praise the name of the Lord with a song; I will magnify Him with thanksgiving". Because He is Lord of all.
Psalm 69:30

Confession

I confess that the old man tries to creep back. These have been times when I let my will rule. Forgive me, I pray, let my will be made null, that I may seek Your will for my life.

Thanksgiving

With a heart of gratitude, thank You Lord Jesus, for removing the stony heart, and giving me a heart of flesh; that I may pursue You and learn to walk in Your statutes.

Supplication

Lord, I cry out to You;
Make haste to me;
Give ear to my voice when I cry out to You.
Let my prayer be set before You as incense,
The lifting up of my hands as the evening sacrifice.
Psalm 141:1-2

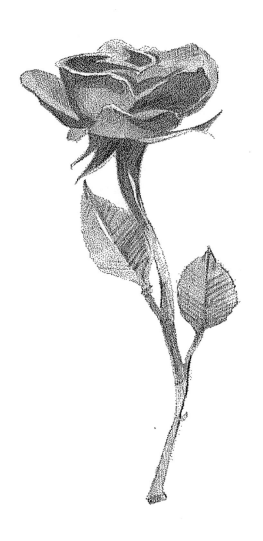

Adoration

Just as a waterfall supernaturally falls without pausing or without slowing down, so does my love for You continue to grow supernaturally. Just as the waterfall cannot be stopped, neither will my love for You. For You are my love, my love supreme.

Confession

In times of hardships, I have allowed trouble, distress and persecution to draw my eyes away from You and separate me from Your love. God, forgive me and give me an undivided heart.

Thanksgiving

Yet in all the things we are more than conquerors, through Him who loved us, because we are victorious in Christ Jesus.
Romans 8:37

Supplication

In the name of Jesus, teach me to stand on God's word in the face of challenging circumstances.

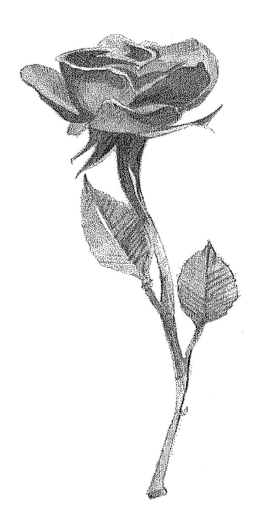

Adoration

You are my lifeline, all my dreams, hopes, needs, and desires lie in You. I only want what You want for me. I love You just that much.

Confession

You are Lord over my life. Your forgiveness of my sins has given me life and made me whole. Give me, I pray, a forgiving heart that I may be an example of Your supreme love.

Thanksgiving

When I reflect on Your goodness, I am overwhelmed with thankfulness, for You have done great things for me. Thank You for my hills and my valleys, thank You for strengthening me as I climb my mountains, and see you at the top beckoning me to come.

Supplication

Help me to see my greatest need is Jesus.

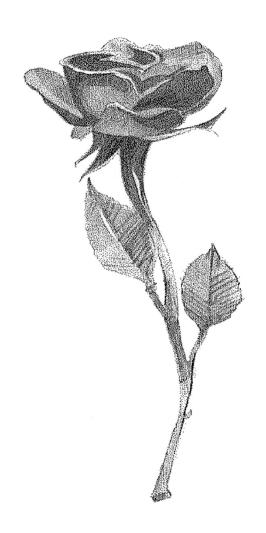

Adoration

Because Your loving kindness is better than life. My lips shall praise You. Thus I will bless You while I live: I will lift up my hands in Your name.
Psalm 63:3

Confession

I have sinned greatly in what I have done, but now, I pray, O Lord take the iniquity of Your servant, for I have done very foolishly.
II Samuel 24:10

Thanksgiving

Thank You for keeping, protecting, loving, sustaining, and filling me. Thank You for making Your purpose clear to me. Thank You for bringing me to a new place in You.

Supplication

Give me, I pray, a holy desire to live a holy life. I earnestly petition You to give me the spirit of wisdom and revelation in the knowledge of You, that I may walk pleasing in Your sight.

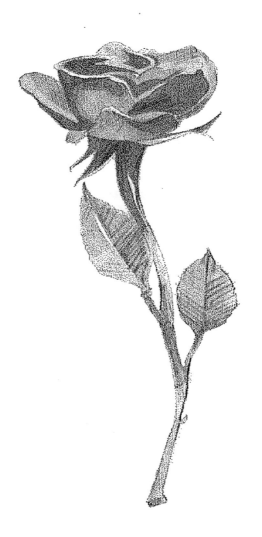

Adoration

As I watch each tender snowflake fall to the ground, I try to measure Your love for me. And yet, not even the blanket of snowflakes stretching across the nation begin to measure Your love for me. Father, no one knows the height nor depth of Your love for us, for it is awesome and immeasurable.

Confession

Lord, I confess that I want to know You more intimately. Help me to live out the spiritual disciplines, that my relationship with You will point others to Christ.

Thanksgiving

May we be strengthened with Your might that we may become mighty in the things of God through Your Holy Spirit.

Supplication

Fill me, O God with all Your fullness until I am complete in You.

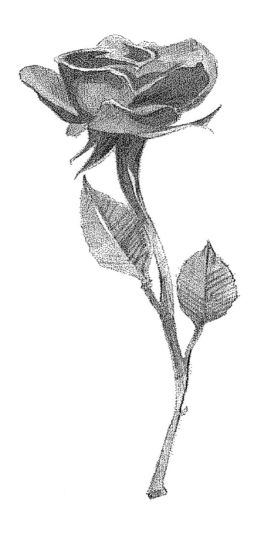

Adoration

The heavens declare the glory of God; Your marvelous works
are proclaimed throughout the universe. The works of Your
hands, and the words from Your mouth, cannot begin to tell of
Your awesomeness.

Confession

I confess, blessed is he whose transgressions are forgiven,
whose sin is covered.
Blessed is the man whose sin the Lord does not count against
him, and in whose spirit there is no deceit.
Psalm 32:1-2

Thanksgiving

For gifts, talents, skills and abilities that You have so
graciously endowed me with, I will use them to offer thanksgiving and bring glory to Your name.

Supplication

Be with me until my days come to an end, on this earth. Bless
me to be the salt that you created me to be. Let me bring flavor
to the earth through good works.

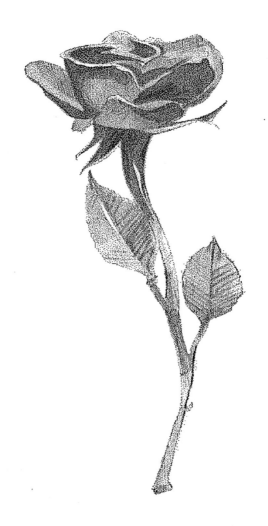

Adoration

Open my lips and my heart, that my mouth may declare Your praises, from the rising of the sun till the going down of the same. I will praise You with my whole heart, O Lord.

Confession

Forgive me when I have been unlovable, unteachable, unaccountable, unkind, and uncontrollable in my behavior, when I have acted like a spoiled brat and caused You to cringe with shame that You made me.

Thanksgiving

Thank You for a love that is persistent and unwavering. A love that is faithful and new every morning, even when I am not deserving.

Supplication

Restore us. O God, cause Your face to shine, and we may be saved.
Psalm 80:3

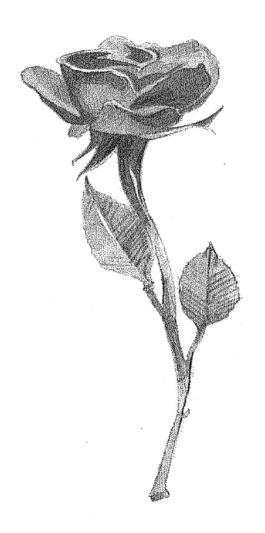

Adoration

Praise the Lord!
For it is good to sing praises to our God; For it is pleasant, and praise is beautiful. I praise You with my lips, my heart, my hands, my feet shall carry the good news of Your love, mercy, and grace. I will exalt You among the heathen.

Confession

My mind is renewed in the word. I bring to remembrance things that are pure, lovely and of good report. Things that will cause my spirit to soar upward.

Thanksgiving

Thank You for giving us the power to choose life or death. Thank You for opening doors no man can shut. Thank You that we are blessed and not cursed. Thank You that the choice is ours to choose life more abundantly.

Supplication

Have mercy on us; O Lord, have mercy on us! For we are exceedingly filled with contempt. Our soul is exceedingly filled with scorn of those who are at ease with the contempt of the proud.
Psalm 123:3-4

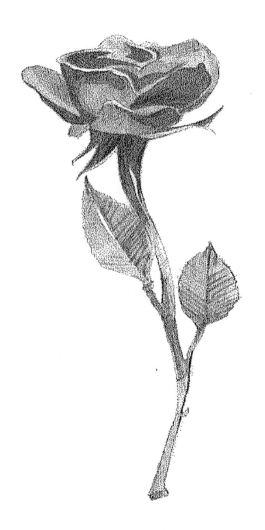

Adoration

For Your mercy that You so graciously give us, moment by moment, hour by hour, day by day. Your mercy carries us through our mistakes, blunders and failures. We praise You our God.

Confession

Deliver us from temptations that would attempt to draw us away from You. Help us to resist the pleasures that the world has to offer. Turn our hearts toward You, my God, my strength, and my redeemer.

Thanksgiving

Thank You, that your grace is sufficient.
Thank You, that in our weakness we are made strong.
Thank You for the confidence that we can do all things through Christ who strengthens us.

Supplication

Lift me I pray, above the temptations that lurks to ensnare me in Jesus' Name.

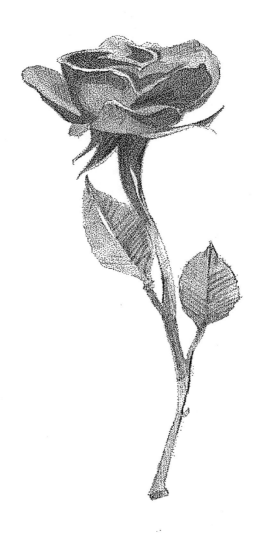

Adoration

You are always available to me, You are always with me, You always hear my cry, You always guide and protect me, You are my silent partner. You are the shadow I cannot see. You are the warmth that envelopes my whole being, I adore You.

Confession

Lord, sometimes when I can't see or hear from You, I get a little shaken. Give me the faith to believe even when you are silent or even hiding.

Thanksgiving

How can I say thank You for the things You have done for me. You have given me new life, new hope, a new song, and a new heart of gratitude.

Supplication

Fill my heart "Jesus" with more of You.

Adoration

You are great, and do wondrous things, You alone are God.
Teach me Your way, O Lord, I will walk in Your truth; unite
my heart to fear Your name. I will praise You, O Lord my God,
with all my heart, and I will glorify Your name forevermore.
Psalm 86:10-12

Confession

Everyday I will bless You and I will praise Your name forever
and ever. Great is the Lord, and greatly to be praised. His
greatness is unsearchable.
Psalm 145:2-3

Thanksgiving

It is good to give thanks to the Lord, and to sing praises to Your
name, O most High; to declare Your loving-kindness in the
morning and your faithfulness every night.
Psalm 92:1-2

Supplication

Enable me to produce a good harvest from the seed I plant
today, help me to keep my faith alive and active, always affirm-
ing that I can do nothing without You, but that I can do all
things through Christ who strengthens me.

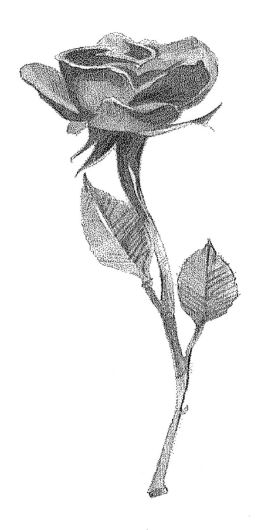

Adoration

My heart is steadfast, O God, my heart is steadfast, I will sing
and give praise.
I will praise You, O Lord among the peoples, I will sing unto
You, among the nations.
Psalm 57:7,9 (NIV)

Confession

Forgive me for the offences of this day, even the ones also that I
am not aware of. Forgive me for the little foxes of evil.

Thanksgiving

I asked and You answered, asking nothing in return. Only You
could love me so completely, asking nothing, but waiting
gently for me to run into Your arms to welcome me into Your
kingdom. Thank youLord.

Supplication

Empower me to become the Proverbs 31 woman, whose worth
is far above rubies and lacks nothing of earthly value. Help me
to be defined in You.

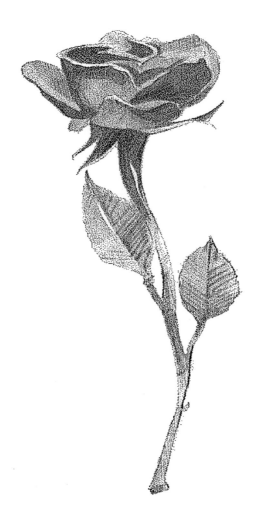

Adoration

Worthy is the Lamb who was slain to receive power and riches and wisdom and strength and honor and glory and blessing.
Rom. 5:12

Confession

Pride You hate, forgive my high looks, forgive me for thinking myself better than others. Rather, I will esteem others higher than myself. I will exhort my brothers and sisters in Godly love.

Thanksgiving

Giver of all gifts, I thank You.
For the gift of laughter, I thank You.
For the gift of tears, I thank You.
For the gift of love, I thank You.
For the gift of prayer, I thank You.
For the gift of family, I thank You.
For the gifts of talents and abilities, I thank You.
For the ultimate gift, "Your Son" I thank You.

Supplication

O Lord, Save my family, friends, neighbors, and co-workers that we may meet in eternity.

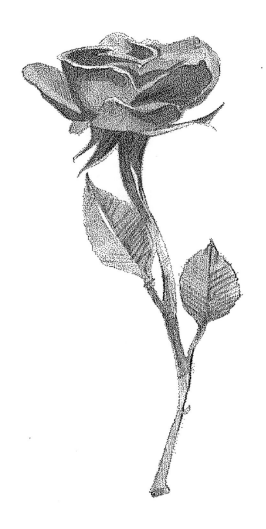

Adoration

There is something about your name that is transcendent. Your name when spoken or thought blesses me, therefore I will extol You, my God and King and bless Your name, forever and ever. The name that is above every name "JESUS."

Confession

There are times when my heart is hardened. Breathe on me Lord. Let your spirit fall afresh on me. Create in me a clean heart, renew in me a right spirit.

Thanksgiving

Now thanks be to God who always leads us to triumph in Christ Jesus, and through us diffuses the fragrance of His knowledge in every place.
II Cor. 2:14

Supplication

Deliver me O God, from self-rule. Give me a spirit of obedience. Through Your Holy Spirit teach me to cast down every high thing that exalts itself against the knowledge of God, bringing every tought into captivity to the obedience of Christ.
II Cor. 10:5

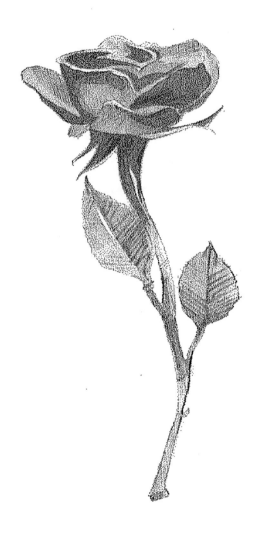

Adoration

Most High God, I magnify You, I glorify You, I exalt You, I praise You, I esteem You, I extol You, O King, I will bless Your name forever and ever, because You are worthy of all the honor and glory.

Confession

Forgive us our debts as we forgive our debtors, and do not lead us into temptation, but deliver us from the evil.
Matthew 6:12

Thanksgiving

O give thanks to the Lord, call on his name.
Make known His deeds among the people.
Sing to Him. Sing praises to Him.
Tell of all His wonderful works.
Glory in His holy name.
Isaiah 12:4

Supplication

Give ear O Lord to my prayer. And attend to the voice of my supplication. In the days of my trouble I will call upon You, For You will answer me.
Psalm 86:6-7

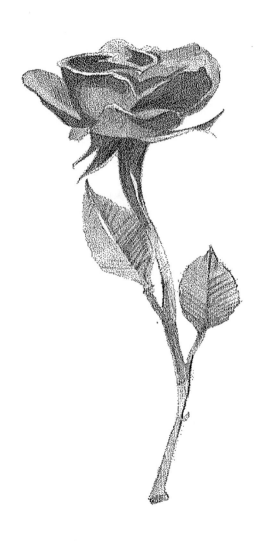

Adoration

My lips will greatly rejoice when I sing to You, and my soul
which You have redeemed. My tongue also shall talk of Your
righteousness all the day long.
Psalm 71:23-24

Confession

When my tongue has tasted evil and my lips have spoken
deceit, forgive me, O God let me depart from evil and do good,
guide me to seek peace and to pursue holiness and wholeness
in You.

Thanksgiving

Thank You, that salvation comes from You. Thank You that we
are not without hope. Thank You, for being my defense. Thank
You that You are not moved, except by faith, prayer and
compassion.

Supplication

Deliver me, O Lord from my enemies;
Teach me to do Your will;
Your spirit is good.
Lead me in the land of uprightness
Revive me, O Lord for Your name's sake
For Your righteousness' sake
Bring my soul out of trouble.
Psalm 143:9-11

The Lifestyle of Prayer

Getting Started

Habit - an established trend of the mind or character, acquired through repetition.

Getting started you would want to choose a quiet place where there are no interruptions, a place you would come daily, preferably at the same time. Coming with the expectancy of meeting the supreme deity, "God." You will need a Bible with a concordance and a worship resource (optional). Using your Bible to find verses until the habit is formed and you begin to pray from the spirit your own prayers of adoration confession, thanksgiving and supplication. Once you acquire the desire of focusing on the Most High God, and His goodness, the desire becomes a discipline, the discipline then becomes a delight. Then you begin to notice there is a constant longing to be in the company of the Holy One. As the Prayer Habit becomes formed in you, guess what? So does the image of Christ.

Prayer Habit Starters

Adoration

Psalm 103:1,2
Psalm 98:1
Psalm 145:2,3
Revelation 5:12,13
I Chronicles 29:11

Confession

Psalm 69:5
Psalm 103:1-6
Psalm 51:3
Romans 7:18
Psalm 32:5

Thanksgiving

Psalm 100:4
Psalm 92:1,2
Psalm 107:1
II Thessalonians 1:3
I Chronicles 16:8-10

Supplication

Psalm 71:1,2
Psalm 51:12
Psalm 98:6,7
Psalm 30:8,10
Psalm 17:8,9

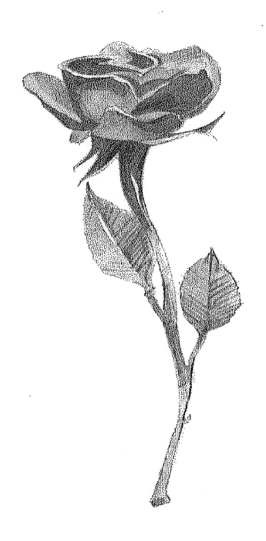

Adoration

_____

_____

_____

_____

Confession

_____

_____

_____

_____

Thanksgiving

_____

_____

_____

_____

Supplication

_____

_____

_____

_____

Adoration

_____

_____

_____

_____

Confession

_____

_____

_____

_____

Thanksgiving

_____

_____

_____

_____

Supplication

_____

_____

_____

_____

Adoration

_____

_____

_____

_____

Confession

_____

_____

_____

_____

Thanksgiving

_____

_____

_____

_____

Supplication

_____

_____

_____

_____

Adoration

_____

_____

_____

_____

Confession

_____

_____

_____

_____

Thanksgiving

_____

_____

_____

_____

Supplication

_____

_____

_____

_____

Adoration

_____

_____

_____

_____

Confession

_____

_____

_____

_____

Thanksgiving

_____

_____

_____

_____

Supplication

_____

_____

_____

_____

Adoration

_____

_____

_____

_____

Confession

_____

_____

_____

_____

Thanksgiving

_____

_____

_____

_____

Supplication

_____

_____

_____

_____

Adoration

_____

_____

_____

_____

Confession

_____

_____

_____

_____

Thanksgiving

_____

_____

_____

_____

Supplication

_____

_____

_____

_____

Adoration

_____

_____

_____

_____

Confession

_____

_____

_____

_____

Thanksgiving

_____

_____

_____

_____

Supplication

_____

_____

_____

_____

Adoration

_____

_____

_____

_____

Confession

_____

_____

_____

_____

Thanksgiving

_____

_____

_____

_____

Supplication

_____

_____

_____

_____

Adoration

_____

_____

_____

_____

Confession

_____

_____

_____

_____

Thanksgiving

_____

_____

_____

_____

Supplication

_____

_____

_____

_____

Adoration

_____

_____

_____

_____

Confession

_____

_____

_____

_____

Thanksgiving

_____

_____

_____

_____

Supplication

_____

_____

_____

_____

Adoration

_____

_____

_____

_____

Confession

_____

_____

_____

_____

Thanksgiving

_____

_____

_____

_____

Supplication

_____

_____

_____

_____

Adoration

_____

_____

_____

_____

Confession

_____

_____

_____

_____

Thanksgiving

_____

_____

_____

_____

Supplication

_____

_____

_____

_____

Adoration

_____

_____

_____

_____

Confession

_____

_____

_____

_____

Thanksgiving

_____

_____

_____

_____

Supplication

_____

_____

_____

_____

Adoration

_____
_____
_____
_____

Confession

_____
_____
_____
_____

Thanksgiving

_____
_____
_____
_____

Supplication

_____
_____
_____
_____

Adoration

_____

_____

_____

_____

Confession

_____

_____

_____

_____

Thanksgiving

_____

_____

_____

_____

Supplication

_____

_____

_____

_____

Adoration

_____

_____

_____

_____

Confession

_____

_____

_____

_____

Thanksgiving

_____

_____

_____

_____

Supplication

_____

_____

_____

_____

Adoration

_____

_____

_____

_____

Confession

_____

_____

_____

_____

Thanksgiving

_____

_____

_____

_____

Supplication

_____

_____

_____

_____

Adoration

_____

_____

_____

_____

Confession

_____

_____

_____

_____

Thanksgiving

_____

_____

_____

_____

Supplication

_____

_____

_____

_____

Adoration

_____

_____

_____

_____

Confession

_____

_____

_____

_____

Thanksgiving

_____

_____

_____

_____

Supplication

_____

_____

_____

_____

Adoration

_____

_____

_____

_____

Confession

_____

_____

_____

_____

Thanksgiving

_____

_____

_____

_____

Supplication

_____

_____

_____

_____

Adoration

_____

_____

_____

_____

Confession

_____

_____

_____

_____

Thanksgiving

_____

_____

_____

_____

Supplication

_____

_____

_____

_____

Adoration

_____

_____

_____

_____

Confession

_____

_____

_____

_____

Thanksgiving

_____

_____

_____

_____

Supplication

_____

_____

_____

_____

Adoration

_____

_____

_____

_____

Confession

_____

_____

_____

_____

Thanksgiving

_____

_____

_____

_____

Supplication

_____

_____

_____

_____

Adoration

_____

_____

_____

_____

Confession

_____

_____

_____

_____

Thanksgiving

_____

_____

_____

_____

Supplication

_____

_____

_____

_____

Adoration

_____

_____

_____

_____

Confession

_____

_____

_____

_____

Thanksgiving

_____

_____

_____

_____

Supplication

_____

_____

_____

_____

Adoration

_____

_____

_____

_____

Confession

_____

_____

_____

_____

Thanksgiving

_____

_____

_____

_____

Supplication

_____

_____

_____

_____

Adoration

_____

_____

_____

_____

Confession

_____

_____

_____

_____

Thanksgiving

_____

_____

_____

_____

Supplication

_____

_____

_____

_____

Adoration

_____

_____

_____

_____

Confession

_____

_____

_____

_____

Thanksgiving

_____

_____

_____

_____

Supplication

_____

_____

_____

_____

Adoration

_____

_____

_____

_____

Confession

_____

_____

_____

_____

Thanksgiving

_____

_____

_____

_____

Supplication

_____

_____

_____

_____

Adoration

_____

_____

_____

_____

Confession

_____

_____

_____

_____

Thanksgiving

_____

_____

_____

_____

Supplication

_____

_____

_____

_____

Adoration

_____

_____

_____

_____

Confession

_____

_____

_____

_____

Thanksgiving

_____

_____

_____

_____

Supplication

_____

_____

_____

_____

Adoration

_____

_____

_____

_____

Confession

_____

_____

_____

_____

Thanksgiving

_____

_____

_____

_____

Supplication

_____

_____

_____

_____

Adoration

_____

_____

_____

_____

Confession

_____

_____

_____

_____

Thanksgiving

_____

_____

_____

_____

Supplication

_____

_____

_____

_____

Adoration

_____

_____

_____

_____

Confession

_____

_____

_____

_____

Thanksgiving

_____

_____

_____

_____

Supplication

_____

_____

_____

_____

Adoration

_____

_____

_____

_____

Confession

_____

_____

_____

_____

Thanksgiving

_____

_____

_____

_____

Supplication

_____

_____

_____

_____

Adoration

_____

_____

_____

_____

Confession

_____

_____

_____

_____

Thanksgiving

_____

_____

_____

_____

Supplication

_____

_____

_____

_____

Adoration

_____

_____

_____

_____

Confession

_____

_____

_____

_____

Thanksgiving

_____

_____

_____

_____

Supplication

_____

_____

_____

_____

Adoration

_____

_____

_____

_____

Confession

_____

_____

_____

_____

Thanksgiving

_____

_____

_____

_____

Supplication

_____

_____

_____

_____

Adoration

_____

_____

_____

_____

Confession

_____

_____

_____

_____

Thanksgiving

_____

_____

_____

_____

Supplication

_____

_____

_____

_____

Adoration

_____

_____

_____

_____

Confession

_____

_____

_____

_____

Thanksgiving

_____

_____

_____

_____

Supplication

_____

_____

_____

_____

Adoration

_____

_____

_____

_____

Confession

_____

_____

_____

_____

Thanksgiving

_____

_____

_____

_____

Supplication

_____

_____

_____

_____

Adoration

_____

_____

_____

_____

Confession

_____

_____

_____

_____

Thanksgiving

_____

_____

_____

_____

Supplication

_____

_____

_____

_____

Adoration

_____

_____

_____

_____

Confession

_____

_____

_____

_____

Thanksgiving

_____

_____

_____

_____

Supplication

_____

_____

_____

_____

Adoration

_____

_____

_____

_____

Confession

_____

_____

_____

_____

Thanksgiving

_____

_____

_____

_____

Supplication

_____

_____

_____

_____

Adoration

_____

_____

_____

_____

Confession

_____

_____

_____

_____

Thanksgiving

_____

_____

_____

_____

Supplication

_____

_____

_____

_____

Adoration

_____

_____

_____

_____

Confession

_____

_____

_____

_____

Thanksgiving

_____

_____

_____

_____

Supplication

_____

_____

_____

_____

Adoration

_____

_____

_____

_____

Confession

_____

_____

_____

_____

Thanksgiving

_____

_____

_____

_____

Supplication

_____

_____

_____

_____

Adoration

_____

_____

_____

_____

Confession

_____

_____

_____

_____

Thanksgiving

_____

_____

_____

_____

Supplication

_____

_____

_____

_____

Adoration

_____

_____

_____

_____

Confession

_____

_____

_____

_____

Thanksgiving

_____

_____

_____

_____

Supplication

_____

_____

_____

_____

Adoration

_____

_____

_____

_____

Confession

_____

_____

_____

_____

Thanksgiving

_____

_____

_____

_____

Supplication

_____

_____

_____

_____

Adoration

_____

_____

_____

_____

Confession

_____

_____

_____

_____

Thanksgiving

_____

_____

_____

_____

Supplication

_____

_____

_____

_____

Adoration

_____

_____

_____

_____

Confession

_____

_____

_____

_____

Thanksgiving

_____

_____

_____

_____

Supplication

_____

_____

_____

_____

Adoration

_____

_____

_____

_____

Confession

_____

_____

_____

_____

Thanksgiving

_____

_____

_____

_____

Supplication

_____

_____

_____

_____

Adoration

_____

_____

_____

_____

Confession

_____

_____

_____

_____

Thanksgiving

_____

_____

_____

_____

Supplication

_____

_____

_____

_____

Adoration

_____

_____

_____

_____

Confession

_____

_____

_____

_____

Thanksgiving

_____

_____

_____

_____

Supplication

_____

_____

_____

_____

Adoration

_____

_____

_____

_____

Confession

_____

_____

_____

_____

Thanksgiving

_____

_____

_____

_____

Supplication

_____

_____

_____

_____

Adoration

_____

_____

_____

_____

Confession

_____

_____

_____

_____

Thanksgiving

_____

_____

_____

_____

Supplication

_____

_____

_____

_____

Adoration

_____

_____

_____

_____

Confession

_____

_____

_____

_____

Thanksgiving

_____

_____

_____

_____

Supplication

_____

_____

_____

_____

Adoration

_____

_____

_____

_____

Confession

_____

_____

_____

_____

Thanksgiving

_____

_____

_____

_____

Supplication

_____

_____

_____

_____

Adoration

_____

_____

_____

_____

Confession

_____

_____

_____

_____

Thanksgiving

_____

_____

_____

_____

Supplication

_____

_____

_____

_____

Adoration

_____

_____

_____

_____

Confession

_____

_____

_____

_____

Thanksgiving

_____

_____

_____

_____

Supplication

_____

_____

_____

_____

Adoration

_____

_____

_____

_____

Confession

_____

_____

_____

_____

Thanksgiving

_____

_____

_____

_____

Supplication

_____

_____

_____

_____

Adoration

_____

_____

_____

_____

Confession

_____

_____

_____

_____

Thanksgiving

_____

_____

_____

_____

Supplication

_____

_____

_____

_____

Adoration

_____

_____

_____

_____

Confession

_____

_____

_____

_____

Thanksgiving

_____

_____

_____

_____

Supplication

_____

_____

_____

_____

ORDER

To place an order for additional copies of *The Prayer Habit*, fill out and mail the form below and we will process your order immediately.

Qty.	Title	Price	Total
____	*The Prayer Habit Journal*	19.95	____
____	*A Woman's Heart*	8.95	____

	Sub Total	_____
	TN residents Tax 9.25%	_____
	Total	_____

Make checks payable to:

The Lovejoy Collection
P.O. Box 41612
Nashville, TN 37204

Serenity Publishing & Communications
P.O. Box 282282
Nashville, TN 37228

Thank you for your support!

Printed in the United States
16155LVS00002B/115-171